Healing Feelings Series

I0078332

# Teddy the Turtle's Family & Friends

*Adventure Three*

Written by Patrice Joy, MA
Illustrated by Kristen Croxton, BA

Heartlink Creations

*Healing Feelings Series: Teddy the Turtle's Family & Friends– Adventure Three*

Copyright © 2019 by Patrice Joy Harkins - Heartlink Creations

All rights reserved.

This book or any portion thereof may not be reproduced or used in any manner whatsoever without the express written permission of the publisher except for the use of brief quotations in a book review.

ISBN 978-1-7325939-2-3

Library of Congress Control Number: 2018910

Editors: Alida Coughlin, C. J. Wright

Illustrator: Kristen Croxton

Printed in the United States of America
First Printing, 2019

Printed by KDP
Available from Amazon.com, CreateSpace.com, and other retail outlets

Published by Heartlink Creations
Bedford, KY

Inquiries: healingfeelings333@gmail.com

# Acknowledgement

I want to thank my family and friends for the exciting adventures that are incorporated in the Healing Feelings Series. The contents of these were taken from times we shared as they were growing up. The sprinklets and pestlets and puppets were the basis of learning moral values and the power of positive interactions. My family, including five sons Brent, Trevor, Ed, Patrick and Kevin; daughter Lisa; eight grandchildren Tara, Heather, Savannah, Matthew, Cory, Dylan, Elliott, and Abe; and three great granddaughters Ava, Leah and Natalie gave the inspiration for these stories. I am grateful for my four daughters in law, Cindy, Anne, Julie and Shannon and my soul granddaughter, Paige.

Thanks to my ‘soul sisters’ in the Native Women’s Wisdom Circle who have been there for me through thick and thin. My friends Joy, Carol, Carla, Donna, Leslie, Deb and Angela shared love and faith to encourage me. I will always hold Momfeather, Pat, Koon Dog, Amy and Bev most dear in my heart through time.

I offer special thanks to my son Ed and my husband Dan who helped a great deal with the editing and publishing process. I am grateful for the talented illustrators, Kristen and Nancy, who have brought my stories to life in color and form; and for my loyal friends Alida, CJ and the publishers. Without all of you, I couldn’t have finished this project.

**OpenDyslexic font is more easily read**

**by persons with some common symptoms of dyslexia.**

Permission is hereby granted, free of charge, to any person obtaining a copy of the fonts accompanying this license (“Fonts”) and associated documentation files (the “Font Software”), to reproduce and distribute the Font Software, including without limitation the rights to use, copy, merge, publish, distribute, and/or sell copies of the Font Software, and to permit persons to whom the Font Software is furnished to do so, subject to the following conditions:

The above copyright and trademark notices and this permission notice shall be included in all copies of one or more of the Font Software typefaces.

The Font Software may be modified, altered, or added to, and in particular the designs of glyphs or characters in the Fonts may be modified and additional glyphs or characters may be added to the Fonts, only if the fonts are renamed to names not containing either the words “Bitstream” or the word “Vera.”

This License becomes null and void to the extent applicable to Fonts or Font Software that has been modified and is distributed under the “Bitstream Vera” names. OpenDyslexic by Bitstream Vera is a trademark of Bitstream, Inc.

# Invitation

We invite you to enjoy the games, puppet shows and learning activities in Book Five. They are designed to increase your fun and help you understand and control your feelings. Experience meeting the Sprinklets personally with relaxing imagery and color.

**See full series and other books by Patrice Joy**

**Healing Feelings Series**

Book 1: Meet the Sprinklets & Pestlets
Book 2: The Sprinklets & Pestlets Take Over Earth
Book 3: Teddy the Turtle's Family & Friends
Book 4: Teddy, Bonnie & the Bullies
Book 5: Play Potentials Booklet
Book 6: Practical Life Skills & Related Research

**Pet Adventures**

Book 1: Buffy Meets Lucky
Book 2: Friends Forever

**Dolphins Dreaming**

**Feather Friends**

**Self Awareness Sprinklet & Pestlet Card**

# Introduction

**This content is designed for those who are elementary school age and older. It's also meant to reach the inner child of those of all ages.**

In this story ten-year-old Teddy shows how being ruled by disruption creates trouble in his relationships. He was so grumpy and snappy that the other kids started to call him Teddy the Turtle. He blamed everyone else for his problems. He argued and fussed a great deal of the time. Teddy demonstrated that moods are contagious and everyone around is affected by them. Teddy realized that he caused a lot of his own problems because he held upsetting pestlet thoughts and feelings. When he began to look at his harmful behavior with honesty, he could correct it and improve his relations. He started doing better with this Mother, his younger sister Tillie and his brother Terry.

This content also emphasizes the power of words and gives tools for change. Hurtful words are called *word attacks*. Pestlet energy hurts those who receive it and brings pain to those who give it to others. Words that are said can't be erased so Teddy begins to think before speaking. As the plot unfolds, it reveals how Teddy improves his life with sprinklet thoughts and feelings. The characters learn gratitude and how to put out a 'heart wish' in a bubble to make their dreams come true.

Bonnie and Teddy enter a doorway in their heart and can see these energetic brain waves. The thoughts a person is thinking regulate these brain waves. The goal is to replace harmful pestlets with positive sprinklets. The characters earn magic star-shaped glasses by being honest. No one can see them, and they give *insight* to see and hear the pestlets and sprinklets.

Teenage Peggy Jo and Dan narrate this adventure story.

Hi, this is Peggy Jo and Dan.

We're going to tell you an exciting story about ten-year-old Teddy. He put himself into one mess after another until he found an easier way to get along.

You may remember from the first two Healing Feelings Adventures that sprinklets are positive feelings and pestlets are pesky destructive ones. What you put out comes back. Teddy certainly learned this lesson.

Watch what happens as his story unfolds!

Teddy was the cutest little boy you could meet, but he could get in the worst moods you've ever seen. He was so snappy that he was given the nickname Teddy the Turtle from bullies at school.

Some of you may understand why Teddy got upset. You may have even felt that way yourself.

Teddy put out pestlets until he found ways to make life better.

Teddy lived with his thirteen-year-old brother Terry, eight-year-old sister Tillie, and their mother. They loved each other a lot but could fight a lot too. I hope your family gets along good.

Dan will tell you how their trouble started one morning.

Early that Monday morning Teddy's mother poked his shoulder to wake him. He slept so sound his safari alarm wouldn't even phase him. Teddy didn't want to get up in the first place, much less be bothered by an elephant trumpeting and a poke in the back.

*No one likes to be poked when they're sleeping*, thought Teddy as he pulled the covers over his head. Angry Pestlet energy was with him.

"Come on, it's time to do your chore and exercise before breakfast," said Mother while she rushed to wake the children. "I want you to wear those nice plaid pants that Aunt Millie gave you for Christmas." Mother paused at Teddy's door and added, "She's coming over this evening and I want her to think you like them." *That is just a little white lie to make someone feel better,* thought Mother.

Dishonesty Pestlet energy was with Mother because she wasn't telling the truth.

"I hate these plaid pants and now I'm going to be teased even more," grumped Teddy. Tillie rushed into his room to make Teddy's bed.

"Get out of here. This isn't your room!" stormed Teddy.

Tillie was just trying to help, but instead Teddy directed his anger at his sister. Angry Pestlet energy was with Teddy.

*No one even cares about my feelings*, he thought as he stormed down the steps.

Angry Pestlet hovered over the whole house. No one saw it, but bad energy was still there. They were all too busy focusing on what each other was doing wrong. Teddy added more pestlets to the morning's problems. He did a lousy job on his chore to prove to his mother he was too young for such hard work. That didn't work with Mother though.

*If I do a sloppy job, I won't have to make my bed and clean the bathroom,* thought Teddy.

The action moved to the breakfast table where Teddy was in trouble.

JUL

Teddy, Terry and Tillie were all in a bad mood at breakfast.

"Why are you being such a pest?" complained Terry. "Just do your work!"

"Shut your mouth. I don't even like you!' yelled Teddy.

Sadness Pestlet joined Terry.

"I was just kidding! Can't you take a joke?" retorted Teddy.

"You shouldn't say mean things." exclaimed Tillie.

They were all too busy focusing on what each other was doing wrong! Guess what happened next... more trouble!

JUL
JUL
JUL

“Now Teddy, I’m not going to have this!” exclaimed Mother. “No employer will put up this laziness when you’re older. Snap out of it, or you’ll be grounded with no allowance today.”

When Mother lectured him this way, Teddy closed his ears. He pulled inside his invisible shell and didn’t hear a word she said. Angry Pestlet grew bigger and turned into Raging Pestlet while it hovered over his head.

Peggy Jo will explain what Teddy did to pass the blame and try to get pity.

Teddy left the house in such an awful mood. He didn't want to go to school so he walked as slow as a turtle. Terry ran ahead, but Tillie stayed with Teddy.

"We're going to be late if you don't hurry," pleaded Tillie.

"I'm tired of everyone telling me I have to snap out of it and go faster," protested Teddy.

"Well, I'm not going to be late!" declared Tillie.

Loving Sprinklet flew over her head because she used self-care and headed on to school.

Bonnie showed up just as Tillie disappeared around the bend of the lane.

"What's wrong?" asked Bonnie.

"The bullies at school are going to make fun of me for wearing these horrible plaid pants. "They'll tease me singing, "Teddy's a turtle. Watch him snap!"

"Don't I know it!" exclaimed Bonnie. 'They sing Bonnie is a dumbo with big ears!' I just wish you wouldn't let the bullies bother you. Why don't you ignore them? That's what I do. Then you can still have a good day."

“Everyone is against me,” whined Teddy. It’s their fault I’m upset.” Teddy wasn’t being responsible for his own actions so Dishonesty Pestlet energy was with him.

He sat there sulking next to Bonnie and Sadness Pestlet. Teddy liked being a victim and he felt pity would bring Loving Sprinklet. Guess What! Pity love is not the same as Loving Sprinklet energy. You have to get sick, or hurt, or mess up your life to get pity love.

Loving Sprinklet is true and pure love energy. It is there for you no matter what!

Bonnie could see the pestlets flying around Teddy by using her magic star-shaped glasses she earned by being honest. No one else could see these magic glasses, but she could see the pestlets and sprinklets with *insight*.

"Are you sure you didn't do anything to cause the pestlet problems today?"

"Well, I was a little grumpy, nothing big," replied Teddy. "Everyone started sending pestlets at me for no reason!"

Kindness Sprinklet energy was with Bonnie. She saw Dishonest Pestlet overhead because Teddy wasn't telling the truth.

Teddy thought for a minute and changed his attitude. *I guess I did do something that could have made them upset,* he thought.

"When Tillie bugged me, I snapped at her. I was angry at Mother and Terry for nagging me, but I sent the anger to Tillie. Sometimes I'm angry at the bullies at school and send the anger to the family at home."

Honesty Sprinklet appeared over Teddy. Guilty Pestlet appeared over Teddy as he realized this was not nice.

Bonnie could see all this with her magic star-shaped glasses. She told Teddy a way to get rid of Guilty Pestlet.

"Take a breath to bring in Kindness Sprinklet energy and let out Guilty Pestlet as you breathe out," said Bonnie.

At that moment Teddy was given magic star-shaped glasses, because he was trying to see the truth in himself and the results of his behavior. The best thing to focus on is sprinklet power. The more of it you have, the more *strength of character* you have.

"You can replace pestlet energy with sprinklets by thinking about us," said Honesty Sprinklet.

"Give thanks for the good things and more good things will come," shared Grateful Sprinklet.

"Think good things about yourself so your heart can fill with love," said Kindness Sprinklet. "The key to sprinklet power is to forgive yourself and to be kind to yourself!"

Stay focused on sprinklet energy and you will draw in all their colors to strengthen you. Then you can have sprinklet power too.

"You can only cross into the sprinklet's World of Magic when you have calm brain waves," said Peaceful Sprinklet. "Pestlets have jagged disrupted brain waves. We do not travel into the jagged brain waves of the pestlet's unhappy world. People can control their brain waves by their thoughts and feelings.

"Breathe in peaceful energy and journey with me to our enchanted World of Magic," invited Peaceful Sprinklet.

"Wow, look at the brilliant colored stars!" exclaimed Bonnie.

"They're everywhere!" gasp Teddy.

"This place is amazing!

"Think of your wish and place it in your heart with sprinklet power. A *heart wish* from Loving Sprinklet can make your wish come true. Magnetic energy of Loving Sprinklet draws your wish or something even better. Call in Peaceful Sprinklet as you send out your *heart wish* and know that what you hope for is on its way to you," said Hopeful Sprinklet.

“We better get going now. Thank you for showing us how to get into the World of Magic,” said Bonnie.

“Remember to make a *heart wish,*” said Hopeful Sprinklet as it soared away leaving a spectacular trail of its healing colors. It formed a rainbow that means the promise of good things.

“It is neat to see the brain waves of sprinklet energy,” said Teddy. *I need to be careful what I am thinking and saying,* he thought.

Dan will tell about the events to come as Teddy went back to his old pestlet ways.

Bully Bill came up the road toward Bonnie and Teddy. He had Raging Pestlet with him. Teddy and Bonnie didn't stay in their sprinklet power. They were drawn into the unhappy world of pestlets by their own fear. They could have taken a deep breath of peace to replace the fear with Peaceful Sprinklet, but they didn't do it.

"Yikes! This energy is terrible!" streaked Bonnie. "Where are we?"

"Oh, no, there's Angry Pestlet flying straight at us," yelled Teddy.

"I'm afraid we're going to be swallowed by pestlet energy!"

“We’re in trouble! I am frightened!” screamed Bonnie.

Fearful Pestlet dove toward Bonnie.

*I can’t let myself follow my fear,* Bonnie thought.

“I have sprinklet power! I am going to stay in Peaceful Sprinklet energy no matter what is going on,” Bonnie declared. “A deep breath of peaceful energy will take me to the peace inside myself.”

That very moment Bonnie was in the Magical World of sprinklets and Teddy was left in the unhappy world of pestlets.

"I feel frightened," cried Teddy. "I'm all alone in this awful place! Where are you Bonnie? It is like I have no control of my thoughts! The words the bullies say to me are getting louder and louder in my head!"

Teddy heard *word attacks* he had said to Tillie and Terry. These came from Angry Pestlet energy.

*I must be worthless if they say so,* thought Teddy.

“I’m here with Grateful Sprinklet.” yelled Bonnie.” I started thinking about what I am thankful to have and want to keep in my life. I started feeling grateful for my family and friends.”

“I’m here too,” assured Grateful Sprinklet,” I’ll never leave you. You were swished into the pestlet’s unhappy world by your own pesky thoughts. Quick, think of something you are grateful to have in your life, Teddy. Then you can return to the sprinklet’s World of Magic with Bonnie.”

Peggy Jo will explain what amazing things began to happen to Teddy.

*I can do it! I am grateful for Mother, Terry, Tillie and Bonnie,* thought Teddy. Poof! When Teddy changed his energy with gratitude, he was immediately joined by three sprinklets.

"I'll connect you to sprinklet power and to your *strength of character*," said Peaceful Sprinklet. "You'll be filled with peace and love. Nothing is stronger than those sprinklets."

Teddy followed this advice in a flash! Whoosh! Teddy was wisped into the sprinklet's World of Magic and was filled with the energy of true, pure love and peace.

They blinked and felt a small jolt. Before they could say zip, bang, doodle, Bonnie and Teddy were standing near their favorite tree.

"Thank goodness you're back!" declared Bonnie. "Promise you'll never let your thoughts and feelings take you away again," said Bonnie.

"I finally see the damage my pestlet energy and *word attacks* caused. It all happened so fast!" replied Teddy in a shaky voice."

His family listened as Teddy told them that he learned the upsetting pestlet energy he had been spreading kept him out of the sprinklet's World of Magic. The family promised to be more loving to each other. Teddy also told them about Bonnie's *heart wish* that everything will work out for the best with the bullies. The family slept better that night and dreamed about sharing sprinklets. You can journey into the spectacular World of Magic too! It can help you have peaceful sleep and remember your dreams. Why don't you try it and get your sprinklet power?

Zzz
Zzz
Zzz

Book Four gets exciting as Bonnie and Teddy use their sprinklet power to deal with the bullies at school. New friends come together to form their own group called Teddy's Team.

## About the Author

Patrice Joy, MA is a licensed interfaith minister and has over forty years of experience in the field of education, business, family dynamics and Integrative Health. Her educational degrees from Antioch McGregor University are a Bachelor of Arts with a double major in Health and Wellness and Human Development and a Master of Arts in Community Change and Civic Leadership. As a Reiki Master Instructor and Herbal Master, she utilizes several forms of vibrational medicine. Patrice has taught at Webster University and Forest Park Community College. She was the first woman hired in territorial sales management for the Xerox Corporation and was hostess of the TV Series entitled *The Parent's Role.* Patrice presented programs for several government agencies including CASA, Head Start, Salvation Army, Fresh Start and One Stop and presented workshops for USAF Falcon Trail Youth Camp, USAFA Family Advocacy and Older Moms Coalition. She was voted Woman of the Year in the Women's Professional Organization in 2011/2012. Her leadership skills have led her to the founding of Creative Learning Programs, Western Celebrations, Seekers of Serenity (SOS) Nonprofit and Harmonizing Health Wisdom.

## About the Illustrator

Kristen Croxton graduated from Hanover College with a BA in Studio Art. She earned the Greiner Award for her senior project entitled Possible Possibilities. This innovative work remains on permanent display. Kristen wants to motivate people to realize the power of art in the healing process and to inspire people to reach their highest potential. Her main life lesson has been to follow her heart and her life path has culminated in a unique blend of Christian Spirituality that honors the teachings of Jesus. She enjoys the psychological aspect of the Sprinklet and Pestlet Series that depicts positive moral values.

Patrice can be contacted at **healingfeelings333@gmail.com**

More information is available at *harmonizinghealthwisdom*

www.ingramcontent.com/pod-product-compliance
Lightning Source LLC
Chambersburg PA
CBHW060756090426
42736CB00002B/55
* 9 7 8 1 7 3 2 5 9 3 9 2 3 *